FRAGMENTS

TALESHA MAYA

<u>FRAGMENTS</u>

First Published in 2018 in Leicester UK by the Soulful Group
a small publishing house with a big purpose
www.soulfulgroup.com

Cover Design by Piu Erminia
Illustrations by Gemma Varney

ISBN-13: **978-1999810436**

DEDICATION

For my Grandad, Ambaram D. Chauhan who instilled in me
courage, integrity and honesty.

ACKNOWLEDGEMENTS

I thank my father for always supporting me in my choices and encouraging me to do what makes me happy. You are the foundation from which I am building my future.

I am grateful for my sister Danni who inspired me to break out of my comfort zone and chase my dreams. I could not have done this without your encouragement and support.

To my brother Anish, I thank you for always pushing me to be a better person and to do better. Your continued support means the world to me.

I thank Kyle for always believing in me and for his encouragement.

Thank you Tash for helping me through all the bad days and
for celebrating the good days with me. I am so grateful
for your friendship.

I would like to thank Shobana for believing in me and my
poems. My gratitude that you chose to publish me.

A huge thanks to Gemma for dedicating her time, energy and
passion to capture my words so perfectly with
her beautiful artwork.

To my family and friends, I value your love, guidance
and support.

ABOUT THE AUTHOR

Talesha Maya is an emerging Leicester based poet and writer who commenced writing at a very young age; she was first featured at the age of 7 in a young writers anthology entitled <u>Hidden Treasures Leicester</u> and the year after in The <u>Hullaballoo Leicester Edition</u>.

At aged 10 she featured in <u>Once Upon a Rhyme East Midlands</u> and finally at aged 12 her poetry was showcased in the East Midlands Edition of <u>I Have a Dream: Words to Change the World</u>.

It seems, she was *destined* to write but her poetry took its current form after the tragic loss of her mother in 2008 and since then she has captured her deeply personal journey from *'grief'* to *'healing'* in a series of poems which have culminated in this first collection.

Her focus is now shifting to identity, culture and politics and her next collection will capture her experiences of being a 'Young British Asian Female'.

In the future, she wishes to expand her writing to highlight the privileges and pitfalls of experiencing love.

She can be commissioned for poetry recitals and writing projects by contacting the Soulful Group.

GRIEF

My Childhood

Emergency calls and frantic voices

In a constant state of sadness and panic

Hospital trips and recovery positions

It was all a bit manic

It's really no wonder I'm having a panic attack

In the quiet moments between the chaos

We sought a bit of normality

We tried to escape reality

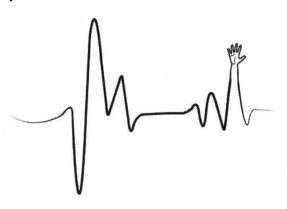

Grief

Like relentless waves dragging you under

Like a winter that never ends

Like a thorn embedded in your heart

A perpetual darkness waiting to engulf you

Goodbye Forever

She flew away in the summer

Little did I know she would never return

Not for another hour, not for another winter

Not for the remainder of my life

Windows to the Soul

Do my eyes tell you my story ?

Of how I've loved and how I've lost

Are they the windows to my soul ?

Do they tell you of the sadness that I hold ?

Survivor

I'm a survivor of childhood trauma

There was a lot of drama

Used to let it haunt me

Wanted to be free

Now it's my fuel

Sometimes my tool

For the poetry, I write

To help me feel alright

At the stroke of midnight

When my mind wanders back

Suicide

I look for answers

To the questions that linger

But she took them with her

When she departed

For Mum

Most nights I lay awake thinking about you

Other nights you're the last thing on my mind

In the divide

The realm between unconsciousness and consciousness

I look for you in the night's sky

An evening star shining brightly

When I wake, your absence consumes me

You are where my mind drifts to

And lingers in spare minutes

Unclear and hazy are my memories of you

Some have even begun to fade

I often think about the words left unsaid

All the memories we had yet to make

The many things you had yet to teach me

All the laughs we had yet to share

All of which I shall never know

9 years

I weep and I wallow

In the sorrow of yesterday

The heavens opened

And the sky cried

It remembered to weep with me for the sorrow we felt

Nine years to this day

Then the sun came out to play

And the grief melted away

Carer

I cared for you, like you cared for me

I bathed you, like you used to bathe me

I fed you, like you fed me

I held you, just like you held me

I felt your pain, like you felt mine

I cried for you like I used to

And sometimes I still do

10 years

I will return

To the place where you rest

Make sure I'm best dressed

Look for a rainbow

Listen to the water flow

Throw in the flowers

I could stand there for hours

Watch them float

Lump in my throat

Follow them down stream

It feels like a dream

To the Grieving

I can't find the words to say

Anything to bring comfort

Or to ease the pain

The grief will still come

And the polite condolences

Will do little to stop your world from spinning

You just have to let it take you where it will

Express what you must

And don't hide behind pretence or bravado

Allow yourself to feel it

Waiting Room

Hours feel like days

Waiting and waiting

It does not seem to end

Hope is fading

I am breaking

Limbo

Stuck in the place between

Neither here nor there

Between consciousness and unconsciousness

Neither living nor dead

Empty

There's a hollow place in between

Where you once lay

5th February 2018

You lie there in your hospital bed

Your body still warm

It's not even dawn

How can you be gone ?

Couldn't you just hang on ?

I thought you'd pull through

I still needed you

And how will I go on without you

You're the one I looked up to

<u>Grieving</u>

Is there happiness after death ?

I'm counting my breaths

Life Goes On

As the sky turns

And the tide returns

Life resumes

The Pain of Loss

I have suffered two great losses in my lifetime

I don't expect you to understand how grief can change a person

You have lost no one

So, you cannot begin to comprehend that kind of pain

And I guarantee if you had you would not be the same either

Gone

I still look for you, sitting in your favourite armchair

But you're not there

I still listen for your voice, singing to your favourite songs

But I cannot hear you

I still make you a cup of tea

Your favourite kind

But it remains untouched

I still think you're here

But you are not

You're gone

Deep Thoughts

Is living really just watching everyone you love slowly die ?

MENTAL ILLNESS

Fine China

Fragile, cracked and broken

Be gentle when you hold me

For I will crumble in your hands

Overthinking

My thoughts cut like knives

Into the thin realms of my self-worth

Eroding my confidence like the sea does a cliff

Bated breaths and rapid heartbeats the soundtrack to my misery

Trying to sleep away the sadness

Ensnared by anxiety

I fear everything

Broken Wings

I want to fly but I have broken wings

Depression

Is it just an imbalance of chemicals in my brain ?

Or perhaps it's my permanent personality

Maybe even a character defect

Could it be the trauma of a childhood of adultness

Or a life lived in sadness

Resilience

It's having a panic attack and then carrying on

Pretending nothing has happened

It's getting on that train and turning up

Even though your brain gives you a hundred reasons not to

It's fighting all those thoughts that tell you that you can't

And that you are not worthy

It's ignoring all your instincts that tell you to run

It's battling all of that every single day

Now that is resilience

Bed

Find me under the covers of my bed

A refuge from thoughts in my head

A shield from anxiety's grip

A temporary fix until it's stripped

<u>Suppression</u>

A scream rising in the back of my throat…

of all the words I have not said,

all the emotions I refuse to feel,

and all the thoughts that are racing in my head…

Floodgate

The floodgates are open

Flowing free and fast

No signs of emotional drought

This bout of sadness so vast

There's no bailout, it's going to last

And cast its shadow over everything

Until only darkness resides here

Hourglass

They say this too shall pass

But how long will it last ?

Anxiety

It's the sweating palms

And the nausea that feels like there is a snake

Squirming around in your stomach

It's the tightening of your chest

And the rapid intake of breath

The flitting thoughts of inadequacy and fear

Fearing death but not really living life

It's the choices and the avoidance of anything that will upset

The fragile balance

The comfort zone of routine and the known

It is the fear of the unknown and the lack of control

Dread

This feeling of dread

It pulls me back to bed

It makes me cry until my eyes are red

Sometimes it makes me wish I was dead

23

Do you know what it's like to be trapped

Trapped by your thoughts…

To be so scared of everything that you can't do anything

This is not how I'd imagined to be at twenty-three

The Revelation

The older I get, the more I understand

Why you choose to die

Rather than to live

Distraction

Disease of the mind

Thoughts so unkind

Help me bide my time

Tight Rope

I walk the line

Telling you I'm fine

This is a delicate balancing act

Can't lose my grip

I don't want to slip

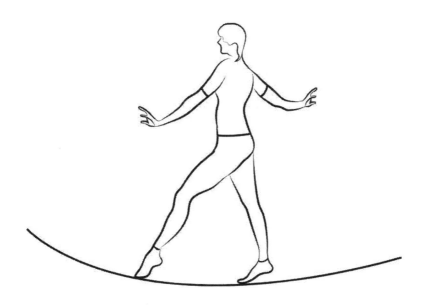

Put Me Back Together Again

Help me I am breaking

Into tiny pieces

And I don't know what to do

Sensitivity

That's the problem you see

I feel too much

Whilst you don't feel enough

<u>Designed</u>

These fragments of mine

Chaotic mind

Thoughts so unkind

It's just the way I was designed

I know I'm pessimistic

And that you detest it

I'll try and change

Because I know our relationship is strained

Poison

Pick your poison

Drink it fast

It'll keep the demons at bay

In a trance, you'll dance

Your head's a mess and your feet will hurt

Lay your head down to rest

Lucid dreams begin, you'll never win

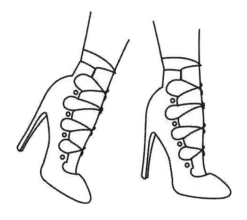

<u>Try</u>

Please don't lose your temper

I really am trying to get better

You tell me it's all in my mind

Well, that's the problem don't you see ?

I know it's hard to comprehend an illness of this kind

I don't expect you to understand me

But I expect you to want to

I expect you to try to

Baptise Me

Let the sea baptise me

Take away my worries and anxieties

Nourish my soul and save my sanity

Skeleton Key

If I seek will I find ?

The master key

To a life of happiness and glee

Oh, I plea with my thoughts to let me be

Just set me free

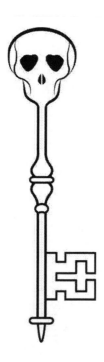

Unravelled

Between the four corners of my room

I lose my mind

Trying to find answers that will not come

Scared to leave my comfort zone

But change will not come from routine and familiarity

I convince myself another day will do no harm

Looking to find motivation

Seeking answers in books

Hanging onto encouragement spoken by others

But this will not provide the answers I seek

Asking myself should I buy a plane ticket

To some foreign land

All to seek what's inside of me

Hoping a change of scenery will fix my mind

And give me a new lease of life

<u>Madrid</u>

I'm scared of change

Find it a bit strange

This foreign exchange

A language gained

Culture explained

Panic remains

Feeling insane

As I try to remain sane in Spain

ANGER

Bled Me Dry

You've drained every essence of my energy

Bled me dry and stole my soul

I'm not a doll

It's taken its toll

You Knew I Was Motherless

You had your chance

Ten years to be exact

To choose to accept

Plenty of time

To mend your ways

And the pain you caused

But you chose to ignore

Instead, reminded me of mistakes I made when I was fourteen

Again, and again

Did nothing but blame

Tortured me with hateful silence

All when I needed your guidance

So, I had to nurture myself

Teach myself

While I longed for your embrace

Now you wonder why I want space

And anger upon seeing your face

Admit It

Have I shamed you ?

Even though I spoke the truth

Maybe you should be ashamed at the way you treated me

You were the adult and I the child

Does it hurt you to see I don't need you ?

What about when you see others take your place ?

Do you regret the way you acted ?

Do you even see the hurt and pain you caused ?

Well, those scars run so deep they'll stay with me forever

Rage

I have a rage that will not be quenched

I stand there rocking on my feet

My fists tightly clenched

With an accelerated heartbeat

A burning and a yearning

To give you a piece of my mind

And it won't be discreet

Because I am hurting

And I am mourning

May this be your warning

For you to retreat

Happy News

Are you mad because I didn't need your approval ?

Or maybe it's because I didn't tell you all the plans I made

I can see it reflected on your face

Like a bitter taste

Your face contorts into a forced smile

You're not on trial

Why can't you be happy for me ?

There's no need to be fake

Perhaps it's too much for you to take

That I can be happy and successful without your help

Well I am and I did it

All by myself

The Aftermath

Red skies

Warning of your demise

I begin to rise

To your surprise

Sever our ties

Cords cuts

Bonds die

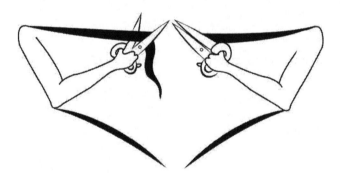

Friendly Enemies

The harshest critics are those disguised as loved ones

They build you up just to break you down

Feigning sweet intentions and best interests

But they prod and poke in all the right places

Waiting for you to draw blood

Under Attack

You put yourself on a pedestal

Whilst you look down on me

Pointing your fingers and pelting your words like bullets

Picking me to pieces, telling me I'm bitter and angry

That I should bite my tongue and mind my body language

So quick to see all the flaws in me

You talk to me about honesty

Oh, the irony when the only honest one is me

Aries

A game of tug of war

With fire under our feet

We dance

Hissing like snakes

Looking to bite

We charge till we meet

Raging rams with entangled horns

Locked into a fight

Hard to beat

An impossible defeat

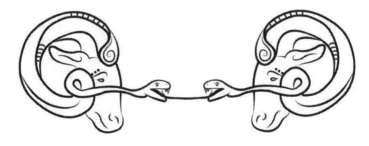

Battle Cry

This is a losing battle

I can hear you cackle as I unravel

You break me so easily

Your words cut so deeply

You have defeated me

Mute

You have shrank me so much that even when I want to scream

I stay silent

Fallout

We fight until it's light

Words cut like knives

Tears run dry

Silence is deafening

Metamorphosis

Why can't you understand

The more you push

The more I shrink

How can I grow when you take away the sun

I need to be nurtured with love and light

Tell Me

You say you'll talk to me

Reveal your troubles and worries

But you seldom do

I never want to pry

Yet I don't want to lie

It's like trying to get blood from a stone

I sigh and I cry

Why do you tell others what you will not tell me ?

Rapid Fire

Sometimes my tongue is quicker than my mind

The words come out like rapid fire

I don't mean to burn

But you should know not to play with fire

Fight Club

Pumped up for the fight

Got me swinging left and right

Ducking down

Dodging blows

Feeling the sting of it

I live for the thrill of it

Toe to toe

Eye to eye

Waiting for the first fist to hit

It's addictive

Chasing the adrenaline

Like a drug

I can't get enough of it

HEARTBREAK

Misery

Just another night staring at these blank walls

Waiting for you to call

It never came

And my heart sank

Cheap flowers and apologies upon your return

Save it all

I can't bear it anymore

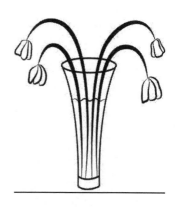

Breaking Point

Join me on the kitchen floor

Let's talk about it all

The tears will pour and our voices will roar

When it's all said and done we'll head for the open door

After Midnight

Tell me your troubles and your woes

In the silence of the night

We can talk until it's light

The Undoing

Bitter are the tears

That roll onto my pillow

As I feign sleep

Silent are the sobs

That escape me

In our room

Which echoes with your soft snores

As you lie oblivious to the hurt you've caused

Long Distance

Wet tears

Warm breath

Just a few minutes longer

Long Embrace

Quick kiss

Big time difference

Short calls

Distance so vast

Closeness so gone

We're strangers again

The Breakup

My words decay in my mouth

I can taste their bitter residue

Things have gone south

In desperate need of solitude

Songbird

And he said:

I'll write you a song just to show you how sorry I am

<u>Fortress</u>

I build my walls high

Cannons ready, bridges drawn

Few enter, many leave

Hard to Love

I am not easy to love

For I was built with prickly skin

And edges so sharp you'll cut yourself trying to hold me

I am not easy to swallow for I am made of fire

I am not easy to tame

For I was raised by wild beasts

Let Go

Slowly I rise out of the darkness

No more cries

Wiped my eyes

Cutting all ties

I've become wise

On to new highs

Shattered Glass

I'll pick up your broken pieces

Hold you in my arms

As I try to put them together again

Love Drought

Wilting flowers

Dried tears

A bin full of tissues

Take away for one

One coffee cup instead of two

An empty space on your side of the bed

Teach Me

Every cloud has a silver lining

But it's hard to see where the good could be in this

I seek and I seek

But I can't find the lesson to be learnt

LOVE

Solitude

Solitude is a friend whom I welcome with open arms. So, you see you are in competition with my love of being alone. You must bring me more happiness than I experience in my own loneliness.

Honey Whisky

Smooth like honey

Sharp like whisky

Ringing in my ears and speaking to my soul

Hypnotising me

I'm under his spell

Life Partner

I don't want to be another one of your conquests

I want to help you

And mould you into a better you

I want to grow together

To be your partner in this crazy thing called life

Venus Fly Trap

Like honey to flies

I wrap you around my fingers

And bend you to my will

Safety Net

On days like today

I want to feel safe in your arms

I want to bury my head into the crook of your neck

To be content and at peace with you by my side

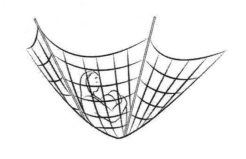

Here with You

We could build forts

Just to feel like we are somewhere else

We could hide under covers

Beneath twinkly lights and patterned sheets

Dear Lover

If you want me to…

…I'll worship you

Love Sick

Sweep me off my feet

Spin me around

Don't put me down

Until I'm dizzy and in need of solid ground

Love

My dark hands

Your pale shoulders

Cocooned around each other

We could stay like this forever

Depth

I want to see into your soul

To know your deepest desires and thoughts

I want to know the essence of your being

Soulmate

Seduce me slowly

Then all at once

First my mind

And my body will follow

Whisper sweetly to my soul

Take my hand and lead me into a new life

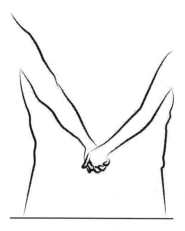

It's You

I am as sure of you

As I am sure that the rain will fall once more

That the tide will return to the shore

That the sun will set and rise again

I am sure of you

Meant to Be

The moon and stars

The ocean and sand

The trees and earth

The sun and the sky

You and I

Bound by something greater

Something the eye cannot see

<u>Vows</u>

I'm forever grateful

Promise to be faithful

I'll always praise you

If you vow not to be hateful

Sunshine

Even in my darkest times you make me happy to be alive

To be in your presence and bask in the light of your soul

I am so blessed to orbit this sun with you

To share this earth with you is the greatest gift of all

Little Sister

Your determination is an inspiration

You could raise a nation

You provide me with a foundation

You give without expectation

You deserve a coronation

Supported me through graduation

Encouraged me with this publication

You help fight discrimination

About to get your fitness qualification

Cause a beauty ideal revolution

What gave you the motivation ?

I've got nothing but appreciation

For my favourite creation

My Father

Who carried me when I could no longer walk,

Who wiped my tears when it all became too much,

Who held my hand and guided me all my life,

Who raised me when my mother could not,

Who taught me when I needed to learn,

Who praised me when I lacked confidence,

Who saw my potential before I ever did…

My hero

Indispensable

You see I was raised by great men

The indispensable kind

Men whose shoulders you could not stand on

Not even with a ladder

So, you see you have a lot to live up to

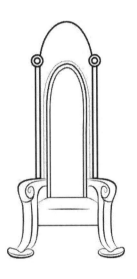

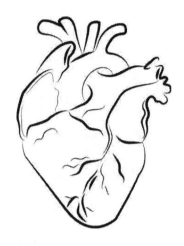

Lullaby

Sometimes I get sad

Sometimes the thoughts get loud

I want nothing more than to crawl into your arms

To lose myself in your kisses for a little while

To listen to your steady heartbeat like a lullaby

Sending me to sleep

Blues

When life's a little blue

I'll call on you

You'll get me through

A few words from you and I'll feel like new

I hope you know I look up to you

Room for You

If my love was the all-consuming kind

I would have enough to swallow mountains

Enough to drain the oceans

To hold the universe inside my heart

And I would still have enough room for loving you

HEALING

Desperation

You seek love and affection in the beds of men

Who are not worthy of you

You rely on others to provide strength and security

You confuse intimacy and attention for love and care

But what you seek is within you

You only have to look deep enough inside yourself

Past the layers of insecurity and fear

My darling you are in desperate need of yourself

Aphrodite and Athena

She is the sun

And I am the moon

She is Aphrodite

I am Athena

We are the same

But entirely different

She shines all day

I shine at night

In the darkness

Where few take notice

Not Her

Too soft for him

Too lost for him

The only type he falls for are the reckless ones

The edgy ones

The girls with chaos in their eyes and emptiness inside

The ones that are so fearless they don't care if they fly or die

A Child of the Ocean

A child of the ocean

I swim at depths you could not reach

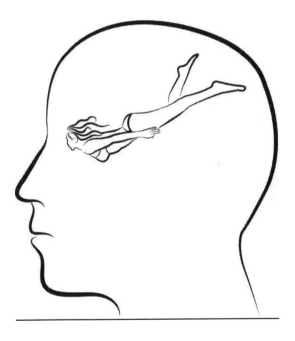

New Me

Shedding the skin

I was once in

The Dwelling

Bury the things that make you sad

Find a place and dig deep

Let the earth swallow your woes

Cover the hole with pretty things

Use flowers and moss to disguise

Sadness now has a hiding place

Change is Coming

I'm about to lose control of everything I know

Time to let go

Try to go with the flow

Release expectations

Put out positive vibrations

Under Construction

I'm working on being better not bitter

To let go of all I hold on to

To live in the moment

To love myself

Be myself

Embrace my flaws

And shadow aspects

Eliminate self-doubt

Be at peace

Break negative habits and thought patterns

Dream big

And recognise I am worthy and deserving

Bloom

I lie awake in my room

Dreaming of all the things ready to bloom

A mental list of all my dreams and desires

Projecting faith onto a higher power

Daughter of the Forest

Twists and turns

Leaves and vines

Roots and shoots

Growth becomes you

Daughter of the forest

Light illuminates you

Even in the darkest corners of your mind

You shall flourish

Like a lotus

Arising through murky waters

You have found yourself

<u>La Loba</u>

My bones shiver and shake

My existential being shifting and changing

The forest is calling my name

Calling out to the wild wolf in me to be set free

I let my feet guide me there

Down the winding paths

Into the deep dark woods

I am home

Why I Write?

I write to release

To express

And to confess

To give me some peace

Keep me sane

And heal the pain

New Book

Turning over new pages

Looking for the same old answers

Will I find what I seek

In the scriptures that I peek at

La Luna

Like the moon

I have craters in my skin

Like the moon

I feel the most in the emptiness of the night

Like the moon

I keep half of myself hidden away

Like the moon

I am rarely whole

My Roots Run Deep

I am not another delicate flower with petals so easy to pick

I am a whole tree with roots that run deep

Don't Forget

Sweet girl why do you worry so ?

You have greatness in your veins and fire in your heart

You are stronger than you believe

For you share the anatomy of powerful beings born before you

A lineage of courageous women

They have lit the path for you to walk

All you need is to let go of your fears

Trust your destiny and the universe

A Love Letter to My Body

I am grateful

For my legs that carry the weight of my body

I am grateful

For my feet which take me down any road I choose

I am grateful

For my arms which allow me to embrace those whom I love

I am grateful

For my hands for letting me write and create

I am grateful

For my stretch marks that remind me how I am changing

I am grateful

For my eyes that allow me to see the beauty of this world

I am grateful

For my ears which let me hear sweet sounds

I am grateful

For my lips that allow me to kiss my loved ones

Beam

I'm radiating gratitude

It's all about that positive attitude

Ensuring your dreams are pursued

Clearing your energy so it's renewed

Projecting intent on a magnitude

<u>Wanderlust</u>

I want to seek adventure

To find the lost part of my soul

Whilst discovering culture, history and nature

Recharge

I feel the earth beneath my feet

Absorb the energy

Anchor me to the ground

Keep me where I stand

As I surrender to the land

Law of Attraction

Feed what you need

Plant the seed

Do a good deed

Breed positivity

About Me

I feel the most alive amongst the trees and green

I become calm at the sound of the sea

I create in the moonlight

I warm under the sun

Inspiration struck

A bit of luck

I've become unstuck

Goodbye Writer's Block

<u>Masterpiece</u>

You adorn your body with flowers and tattoos

Thinking maybe it would make it more beautiful

But you forget your flaws and scars tell stories

More beautiful than art

They tell us of how you became to be who you are

The Art Work is You

Your body is a canvas, your markings are the art

Tree Trunks

If my thighs are trunks, then let my feet be my roots and my body be the tree - let my mind grow and my thoughts blossom

People

The best things in life are people

With beating hearts and infectious laughs

Who pull you from the depths of despair

Back into the light

Purpose

I used to question why life only presented me with hardship

Now I see that all the darkness has led me to the light

It gave me fuel for me to fulfil my purpose

Everything has led to this moment

Of success and abundance

Yin and Yang

I've come to realise that no year is entirely bad

Or entirely good

Each year comes with its hardships

Its battles

Its defeats

Its heartbreaks

But it also comes with

Its wins

Its blessings

With joyous moments and love

Each year you experience a bit of both

The good in the bad and the bad in the good

Seedling

I am love

I am light

Every time you cut me down

I will sprout again

Voice Found

It took me a while to find my voice

But now that I have

I will roar so loudly

The earth will shake

And you will come tumbling down onto your knees

Progress

I used to tremble at the thought of speaking out loud

I would shake, stutter and sweat

I used to obsess over what people would think

Desperate for their approval

I used to hate drawing attention to myself

So I would shrink myself

Now look at me

Look at what I'm about to do